Colour Nature Library

BIRDS

By
BRUCE COLEMAN

Designed by
DAVID GIBBON

Produced by
TED SMART

COLOUR LIBRARY BOOKS

INTRODUCTION

About 150 million years ago the first bird-like creature emerged from reptilian stock. Crow-sized, with long tail and feathered wings, it made the first steps towards the true flight achieved by its descendants by gliding from branch to branch. It possessed many of the features of a reptile, including a long, bony, jointed tail, claws, which were on the wings and assisted climbing, and a jaw full of sharp teeth which indicate that it was carnivorous. In other ways it was more bird-like, being covered with feathers, not scales, and possessing feet designed for perching. A fossil of this bird was found in Cretaceous slate beds in Bavaria and was christened *Archaeopteryx lithographica* by scientists, a name which means 'the ancient winged creature of the stone for drawing'. *Archaeopteryx* first appeared some time during the Upper Jurassic period (150 million years ago) and from that time, through to the Cretaceous period (135 to 70 million years ago), the general development of birds seems to have proceeded very slowly; less than thirty fossil species have been discovered. Nevertheless birds were on the way to becoming the successful and dominant vertebrates (in terms of the number of species) that they are today. The Cretaceous saw the emergence of *Hesperonis*, a diver-grebe which was flightless and between one and two metres in length, *Ichthyornis*, a toothed and tern-like sea-bird, *Parascaniornis*, a primitive flamingo and *Elopteryx*, an ancestor of present-day gannets and cormorants.

During the Palaeocene and Eocene epochs (70 to 40 million years ago) many of our modern birds, such as the ostrich, pelican, duck, wader and raptor, developed. This was also the time of an incredible giant of a bird, the carnivorous *Diatryma*, which was flightless, over two metres high with a head the size of a horse's and formidable bill, and pursued its prey over the open plains on its powerful legs. The Oligocene and following Miocene epoch (about 40 million to 11 million years ago) was a warm period in the history of the earth and saw the appearance of the stork, plover, owl, pigeon, parrot, crow and secretary bird. This was an age of orderly development in the evolution of birds. The Pliocene and Pleistocene epochs (11 to 2 million years ago) were times of change with a cooler climate which preceded the Ice Age. Nevertheless, birds thrived and were at the height of their success with about 11,600 different species, a larger number than there are today.

It has been estimated that the last 140 million years have seen the emergence of a half a million or even a million different species of bird but natural selection and climatic and structural changes over the Earth took their inevitable toll. Bigger changes followed, however, with the emergence of the most highly adaptable and dangerous of all species – man. His evolution was to have a major effect on the bird populations of the world. Man the hunter became man the farmer and builder, man the coloniser, man the industrialist and man the polluter. The impact of this has been so catastrophic that the number of bird species today is about thirty per cent less than in the Pleistocene epoch. First victims were the island species such as the moas of New Zealand, the elephant bird of Madagascar, the great auk of the North Atlantic and the dodo of Mauritius. As they were all flightless they were easy prey to the early mariners. The invention of the gun soon brought much more mobile species within easy range and as a result the most abundant wild bird the world has ever known, the passenger pigeon, was quickly eliminated. It has been estimated that before 1840 there were between 5,000,000,000 and 9,000,000,000 pigeons. Huge flocks would eclipse the sun and one flock, over one and a half kilometres wide, took four hours to pass overhead and was calculated to be nearly 400 kilometres long and to contain 2,230,272,000 birds. Such flocks were easy targets for guns so that by the end of the nineteenth century this pigeon was well on the way to extinction. The last of the species died in Cincinnati Zoo at 1 p.m. on 1st September 1914.

The gun is still with us but in addition there are now the added pressures of world-wide pollution of rivers, seas and oceans and the destruction of natural habitats as well as more local problems such as the bird trapping which occurs on such a massive scale in the Mediterranean. All is not lost, however, for we now have a welcome newcomer on the scene, man the bird-watcher and conservationist. As a result of organised conservation, the lobbying of government agencies and the establishment of reserves and national parks, supported by a sympathetic and educated press, radio and television, public opinion is increasingly on the side of our wildlife. Positive conservation has seen a number of species rescued from the brink of extinction, the nene goose and the trumpeter swan being two good examples. While American conservationists keep an ever alert eye on their whooping crane and Californian condor, Europeans monitor the Scottish osprey and the Spanish imperial eagle. It is our duty to see that they survive, as is their right.

Previous page: Tawny owls.

Left: European stork landing at its nest at sunset.

Robins

The Pekin robin *left* is related not to the robins of the thrush family but to a group of birds known as babblers. This large group is found primarily in the Oriental Region and is also well represented throughout Africa and Australasia. The Pekin robin is a good songbird which is frequently kept in captivity; its natural home is the wooded hills, mountains and forests of the Himalayas, India, China and Burma.

A few years ago British bird watchers elected the robin *right* as their national bird in recognition of its friendliness and long service to British gardeners. This affinity with man is unique to the British race; continental robins are shy and retiring. The robin is a highly territorial bird which defends its territory aggressively against all other robins except its mate. This aggressive behaviour was noted as long ago as the third century B.C. in the phrase 'One bush does not shelter two robins'.

The American robin *below* was originally a species of woods, forest borders and clearings, but with the advent of man it soon occupied the newly-created habitats of gardens, parklands and orchards.

Garden Birds

The mistle thrush (fledgling *top left*, adult *near right*) is Europe's second largest thrush, growing to a length of about twenty-six centimetres. Over the years this species has moved into parklands, villages and large gardens. It is uncertain if it seriously competes with the song thrush and blackbird but it is certainly pugnacious towards them as well as towards other birds. It has been known to kill fledglings and will mob birds larger than itself such as the carrion crow, magpie and jay, and will not hesitate to 'have a go' at human intruders in defence of its nest. This wary thrush does not visit bird tables freely but will be attracted to a garden well-stocked with berries such as mistletoe, holly, rowan and yew. The mistle thrush is widely distributed through Europe and can be found as far east as central Siberia as well as in the western Himalayas, North Africa and Asia Minor.

In severe winters the wren *far right* population can be drastically reduced but a succession of mild winters has been favourable for this diminutive bird and it is now Britain's commonest species. It is also Britain's most widely distributed bird, being found throughout Europe as well as in China, Japan, India and the United States, where it is known as the winter wren. It is a highly adaptable bird; there is hardly a habitat it has not colonised and it is quite at home in gardens, woodlands, on rocky coasts or on mountain tops.

One of America's best known birds is the blue jay *bottom left,* a species of open woodland (particularly oak and beech) which has successfully invaded the parks and suburbs of most North American towns. Blue jays are easily attracted to bird tables. At the end of the breeding season blue jays travel around in small flocks, searching for a variety of food including insects, snails, salamanders, frogs, mice and plant material. They enjoy acorns and beechnuts and bury those they do not eat – many new oak and beech trees must have developed thanks to the activities of the blue jay. This attractive crested bird is found from Newfoundland south to Florida and the Gulf States.

The summer habitat of America's evening grosbeak *bottom right* is the boreal zone of spruce and other conifers. These birds are as big as starlings, are highly gregarious in winter, and will visit feeding stations. Their huge conical ivory-coloured bills crack sunflower seeds easily; these are their favourite table food.

Tits

The name *tit* is an abbreviation of the word *titmouse; tit* means a small object and *mouse* is a corruption of *mase* which is Anglo-Saxon for a kind of bird. Tits are popular birds which are easily trained to come to the hand for food and are among the first to visit a newly-erected bird table.

The blue tit (fledglings *far left*, adults *below*) is a species of woods, copses and hedgerows, parks and gardens. If you provide a bird table with a supply of nuts and cheese it will become a regular visitor; provide a nesting-box and it will become a regular nester. In any case it will probably breakfast on your morning milk delivery. The larger great tit *right* is a frequent visitor to the bird table and is often hostile to its smaller relatives. The long-tailed tit *near left* builds a nest of moss, lichens and spider silk which it then lines with up to 200 feathers. In winter these attractive small birds travel about in small feeding parties. Another visitor to the garden is the coal tit *bottom left*; although it prefers to nest in woodlands it will use boxes if these are placed near the ground.

Songbirds

Few songbirds display themselves as conspicuously as the skylark *left* which delivers its loud and pleasant song as it rises high into the sky. It is a bird of open country, found on grasslands and meadows, which often moves about in flocks outside the breeding season. The bird-watcher will probably also hear the rich warbling song of the shy blackcap *right* before he sees it. Although this bird is primarily a summer visitor to Europe, returning in the autumn to Africa, small numbers do over-winter in Britain and parts of Europe.

Mockingbirds are members of the *Mimidae* family, which includes fine songbirds, many of which are accomplished mimics; the Galapagos mockingbird *below* does not have this ability.

The attractive yellowhammer *far right* is widely distributed in Britain but there is now evidence which suggests that, in England anyway, its numbers are decreasing. The yellow and chestnut plumage and unmistakable song ('a little bit of bread and no cheese') makes this an easy bird to recognise.

Summer Migrants

The house martin and the swallow are two of Europe's best known migrants. They both feed on small flying insects and their dependence on this kind of food means that they have to move south in autumn to the warmer climes of Africa. Both species return the following spring; the first swallows have returned by early April. Before the arrival of man the builder, swallows and martins used cliffs, caves and rock faces for their nesting sites. Now both species are closely associated with man; the martins construct cup-shaped nests of mud lined with feathers under the eaves of houses *left*, swallows build more shallow, almost saucer-shaped, nests of mud, straw and grasses on the rafters of sheds, barns and garages *below left*.

The spotted flycatcher *right* is a bird of open deciduous woodlands, forests, orchards, gardens and parklands. It winters in wooded regions south of the Sahara eastwards to north-west India and arrives in Europe from April to early June. Almost exclusively an insect eater, although it eats berries in the autumn, it takes off from post, wire fence or hanging branch, twisting and turning athletically in pursuit of its prey. In the summer months this species is widely distributed east to Russia and northern Mongolia and south to the Mediterranean.

Wherever it occurs the cuckoo *below and far right* is known by names which all imitate its call. It is called *coucou* in France, *Kuckuk* in Germany, *koekoek* in the Netherlands, *kukushka* in Russia and *kak-ko* in Japan. Only the male makes this call, the female has a less familiar bubbling call. If disturbed in the nest the young makes a low, disconcerting hiss which turns to a whistling scream if it is handled. The cuckoo does not build her own nest but is parasitic on other birds. She restricts herself to a limited territory and a specific host; some females only use the nests of meadow pipits while others prefer those of reed warblers, wagtails, robins and buntings. One cuckoo, observed over a period of fifty days, laid twenty-five eggs in twenty-five different nests, all of which belonged to meadow pipits.

Storks and Cranes

Although they are similar in appearance and shape, the long-legged storks and cranes are not closely related. There are seventeen species of stork and fourteen species of crane and, sadly, the numbers of cranes have fallen so alarmingly low that there is now an urgent need for special protection for them if they are to survive. The numbers of the European or white stork *left* have also decreased in certain parts of Europe but when they migrate it is still possible to see them in their hundreds if not thousands.

One of the most attractive of the crane family is the African crowned crane *right* which inhabits the marshes, swamps and cultivated areas of that continent. During the breeding season pairs or groups perform elaborate courtship dances. These birds are often domesticated to keep down insects and reptiles in African gardens. The sandhill crane *below* has, over the years, been severely persecuted for sport and has disappeared from many parts of its former American range.

Geese

Geese belong to the sub-family *Anserinae* which also contains the swans and whistling ducks. There are fifteen species of true geese, all of which are grass-grazers. Geese are migratory and fly great distances. The cackling Canada goose flies from its breeding grounds on the Alaskan coast to its winter quarters which range from British Columbia to California. The most abundant goose in the United States is the lesser snow goose *left and below left* which can be seen in huge groups cropping pastures or in stubbled fields where they feed on waste grain. These beautiful geese live in the Arctic region from Siberia to Greenland in the summer months but, as the Arctic winter sets in, they make an incredible journey of 4,000 kilometres to the Gulf of Mexico and beyond.

Canada geese *right* are born covered with down, with eyes wide open and the ability to move about as soon as they are dry. They have enormous appetites and, if food is plentiful, can double their weight in a week.

The Arctic coast of Alaska and Siberia is the home of the emperor goose, a species which defends its nest *below* particularly vigorously, but, in spite of this, many goslings are taken by skuas, gulls and owls.

Ducks

The group known as the dabbling ducks contains many of the most popular waterfowl such as mallard, wigeon, teal, shoveler and pintail; all are primarily vegetarian surface feeders although they will dive and up-end for food. The mallard *right* can be found on almost every village or city pond but it is equally at home on estuaries, lagoons and on the shoreline. It is a highly gregarious bird which will flock in hundreds or indeed in thousands. In the west Palearctic the population has been estimated at between four and five million. The exquisite wood duck *left* almost followed the dodo and the great auk into extinction, for the pressures on it during the early part of this century were tremendous. Many of the wooded swamps in which it nested were drained, commercial hunters took their toll and there was a demand for stuffed wood duck to adorn the American home. It is now protected and is probably the commonest nesting duck in the eastern United States. The shoveler *below* is widely distributed throughout the northern hemisphere and is easily recognised, even from a distance, by its over-sized bill.

Swans

There are seven species of swan, the world's largest waterfowl. Five of them, the mute, trumpeter, whooper, Bewick's and whistling, are pure white and are only to be found in the northern hemisphere. The remaining two, the black and the black-necked, inhabit the southern hemisphere.

The whooper swan *above* nests in reed beds and on small islands on lakes in the tundra zones of Norway, Lapland, Iceland, Russia and Siberia and occasionally in Scotland. In the winter it migrates to Scandinavia, the southern Baltic, the British Isles and the Black and Caspian Seas.

At one time the trumpeter swan *top right* population was so low that the species was in danger of extinction. Fortunately active conservation management has saved this North American bird; one of the best places in which to see it is the Yellowstone Park region of Wyoming.

The mute swan *bottom right* is not really voiceless as anyone who has approached its nest and young will know, when the explosive grunt or threatening hiss is quite alarming. In flight its wings make a musical throbbing sound. This century has seen an increase in the British population to a current figure of 1,900 birds and it has been introduced into the United States, being particularly well established on the east coast.

Australia is a continent of unusual and unique creatures so it is perhaps not surprising that it should have a black swan *bottom left*. This magnificent bird has been introduced to many ornamental lakes in the United States, Europe and New Zealand.

Sea-birds

Almost three-quarters of our planet is covered with sea water which provides a habitat for some 260 species of bird. The North Atlantic is the home of the gannet *left,* a bird with a wing span of nearly two metres, which catches its prey, surface fish, after spectacular plunge dives from heights of more than thirty metres. Three-quarters of the world population of about 200,000 pairs is to be found around the British Isles. Gannets nest in colonies of which one of the largest is at St. Kilda and has 52,000 pairs.

There are only three species of tropic-bird; the largest is the red-tailed *right,* a bird of the Indian and Pacific Oceans. These attractive birds are gregarious during the breeding season and have involved aerial courtship displays.

There are thirty species of cormorant, medium to large sized aquatic birds with long necks and bodies which catch fish by diving from the surface and pursuing their prey underwater. The king cormorant *far left* is found in the Falkland and South Georgia Islands. The little white-throated shag *below* is the most widely distributed of the New Zealand fresh-water cormorants and is found on lakes, swamps, rivers and sea cliffs.

Albatrosses

Albatrosses are truly oceanic birds which have an unusual ability to utilise the up-draughts of air rising from the waves; their long narrow wings keep them airborne with little or no movement. These birds can travel vast distances; one individual is known to have travelled 10,000 kilometres from its native area. Albatrosses are mainly nocturnal feeders and their favourite food, cuttlefish and squid, rise to the surface at night.

The best known species is the wandering albatross *right*, an impressive white bird with black wing-tips and a wing-span of about three metres. Most albatrosses nest in colonies; the wandering albatross is no exception and lays a single egg each alternate year.

The black-browed albatross *below and far right* is the most approachable of the albatross family, having little fear of man. It is a bird of the southern hemisphere but from time to time it appears in the North Atlantic and one black-browed albatross joined a gannet colony in the Faroe Islands in 1860 and stayed there for thirty years. The grey-headed albatross *left* also breeds on islands in the southern oceans.

Gulls

Gulls are aggressive, adaptable, predatory, scavenging birds. There are forty-three species of them which include sea birds, land birds and even town birds. Mixed flocks follow fishing boats for scraps *right* or follow ploughs, feeding on worms and other invertebrates, as are these black-headed gulls *bottom right*. Most European towns and cities support a population of these small gulls which scavenge around lakes, ponds and rubbish tips. In the summer, after changing into their dark-headed breeding plumage *left,* they nest in colonies which vary in size from very few to up to 12,000 pairs. The black-headed gull is widely distributed throughout Europe and Russia and occasionally turns up in the United States.

The larger, more robust, herring gull *below* is found on both sides of the North Atlantic and has greatly increased in numbers during this century. During the period 1900-65 the New England population increased from between 4,000 and 8,000 pairs to between 110,000 and 120,000 pairs. This species quickly utilises new man-made sites and nests on bridges, piers and roof tops.

Terns

Terns are related to the gulls but are finger-winged and more slender-bodied birds; most species are confined to the tropics, where they probably evolved. They can be conveniently separated into two groups – the marine species, which are white-bodied and black-capped (during the breeding season) and the marsh species, which have a preponderance of black in their plumage and nest on salt and fresh-water marshes. Terns dive for their food or pluck it from the surface of the water. The sooty tern *below* is an extraordinary bird for one so pelagic for it cannot land on water because its feathers are not waterproof. When feeding it hovers or swoops before grabbing small fish or squid from the surface of the water.

Common Terns *left* nest in a variety of places including beaches, sand-dunes, marshes and gravel pits. They have even been observed nesting up river valleys in Scotland. Adult birds defend their nests aggressively against all predators, whether man, fox, weasel, rat or gull. The elegant tern *right* is a large bird which breeds in colonies in the southern United States, Mexico, West Indies, South America and West Africa.

Auks

Auks are chunky diving birds of the northern hemisphere which, like another ancient group, the penguins, 'fly' underwater. They are often described as the penguins of the north, but are not related to penguins. In historic times the great auk, the largest of the family which stood nearly a metre high but could not fly, has become extinct. Great auks were slaughtered in their thousands, their eggs were gathered in enormous numbers; inevitably the species became a rarity with a price on its head, hunted avidly by collectors. On 3 June 1844 the last pair of great auks was killed in Iceland; on 5 March 1971 a stuffed specimen (in breeding plumage) was sold at Sotheby's for £9,000.

The commonest seabird in the North Atlantic is the puffin *top and bottom right*, there being nearly half a million birds in Britain and Iceland alone. Puffins dive for their food using their wings for propulsion and their feet as rudders. As many as ten fish can be held cross-wise in their colourful bills. The brightly-coloured red, yellow and blue beak is a breeding adornment which is thrust at its neighbour in a form of threat display or is used in courtship with much bill-rubbing which strengthens the pair bond. In the post-nuptial moult the brightly-coloured horny plates are shed. Puffins return to their colonial nesting sites in March and April. They nest in burrows which they excavate in the soft ground of cliff tops or banks; the beak is a most useful tool for this purpose.

A distinctive feature of the razorbill is its deeply compressed beak which is crossed with a white line. This is capable of holding several fish *far left*; a maximum of nine has been observed although five or six are more usual. Like other auks, its flight is direct with rapid whirring wing-beats; when landing on a cliff ledge the feet are splayed out in a braking action *near left*. This species is strictly endemic to the North Atlantic, being found on the coasts of eastern North America south to Maine as well as in Greenland, Scandinavia, Iceland and the British Isles.

Guillemots *below left* are highly gregarious birds in the breeding season when they gather together in enormous numbers; one colony was estimated to contain 70,000 pairs. Guillemots can be distinguished from razorbills by their slimmer build and slender-pointed black bills.

Penguins

The seventeen or eighteen species of penguin are well adapted to life in the inhospitable waters and icy wastelands of the southern hemisphere. Their bodies are insulated against the extreme cold by close-packed feathers and the modified wings (flippers) are strong and narrow, enabling the birds to cut through the water at speeds of ten knots or more so that they can obtain enough propulsion to leap about two metres out of the water in order to land on ice shelves or rocks.

The two largest species, the king *overleaf, right* and the emperor, do not make nests but incubate their single eggs by resting them on the top of their feet and covering them with warm belly skin. Although females do share in the incubation the males take the major share of this work, incubating for something over sixty days, during which period they shed over a third of their body weight. The eggs must not be exposed to the cold for more than a moment for the embryo would die within seconds.

The Adélie penguin *overleaf, top left,* is the most common penguin species and there may be up to a quarter of a million birds in its colonies or rookeries, all jostling and squabbling for mates and nest-sites. Having selected a site, Adélie penguins spend much time in their 'ecstatic' displays, when heads and necks are stretched vertically while flippers are beaten slowly and braying calls are emitted. The nest is built from pebbles which are collected by the male and dropped at the feet of the female; during this procedure they bow and nod to each other as if in greeting. The female lays her two large eggs on the nest before going off to sea and leaving the male to the task of incubation, which takes about six weeks.

The gentoo penguin *overleaf, bottom left* has a circumpolar distribution, nesting in the Falklands, Kerguelen, Macquarie, South Georgia and other small Antarctic islands. The chinstrap penguin *left* is common in the Antarctic Peninsula, South Orkneys and South Shetlands and appears to be enlarging its range. Rockhopper penguins *bottom right* are not only found around many of the Antarctic islands but also breed in New Zealand, Tristan da Cunha and the Falkland Islands. The orange-yellow head-plumes of the macaroni penguin *top right* are a distinctive feature of this species which nests on many of the sub-Antarctic islands.

Pelicans

Pelicans are among the largest of birds and are widely distributed in temperate and tropical regions. They have a long history dating back thirty or forty million years. They are primarily fish-eaters and are well known for their huge bill-pouches into which they scoop their food. There are eight species of pelican, all of which are gregarious in both breeding and feeding habits. They are strong flyers but flocks will often circle lazily on rising thermals, so achieving a great height.

The Dalmatian pelican *right* is also known as the crested pelican because of the curly feathers on its head and nape. It is a bird of marshy shores of lakes, deltas, inland seas and large rivers, found locally in south-eastern Europe from Albania and southern Macedonia to northern Greece and in the coastal regions of Rumania and Bulgaria, Russia and Mongolia. In recent years there has been a decline in the population as marshes are drained and as the central Asiatic lakes gradually dry up. A hundred years ago there were at least 300,000 Dalmatian pelicans on the Danube delta yet by the early 1960s the population was

down to 2,000. They often fish in organised flocks of about one hundred birds which splash and paddle rapidly, driving shoals of fish into shallow water where they can be encircled and caught.

The pink-backed pelican *top left* is a bird of tropical Africa found on both alkaline and freshwater lakes, in bays, harbours and mangrove swamps, and even in grasslands where it feeds on locusts. These pelicans frequently nest well away from their feeding grounds – sometimes the two areas are as much as sixty kilometres apart.

The white pelican *below right* of Europe, Asia and Africa, is the second largest species of pelican. This bird also fishes in cooperative flocks, the huge pouched bills, each of which can hold nearly fifteen litres of water, scooping up the fish that have been trapped. White pelicans nest in colonies with 300–40,000 birds at one site.

The coastal regions of North and South America are the home of the brown pelican *below left*, which is a spectacular dive-bomber. When fishing, small flocks fly eight to ten metres above the surface of the water, from which height they watch for food; having located it they twist sharply, with half-closed wings, and plunge with an enormous splash into the water.

Flamingos

Flamingos are gregarious wading birds of warmer regions which haunt brackish and salt water lakes where there is plenty of food – microscopic algae, worms and insect larvae. In order to extract this minute food from the water the beak *left* has evolved into a very efficient pump containing laminae which act as filters and trap the edible material as the muddy water is passed through.

The greater flamingo *right* breeds in isolated colonies in southern Europe, on the lakes of Africa's Rift Valley, in the Caribbean and in South America. The Camargue area of France has a famous colony which appears to have become established during the early part of this century; the numbers have varied from under 2,000 up to about 8,000 pairs. In East Africa the greater flamingo breeds at any time of the year, shaping a mound of mud into a flattened cone for use as a nest into which a single egg is laid. The grey downy chicks are fed on a regurgitated soup-like substance. The lesser flamingo *below* is the most numerous of all the flamingos; there are about three million of them living in the East African lakes.

Plovers

All plovers are ground-nesting birds which rely on camouflage or distraction displays to escape the many predators which threaten their vulnerable nest sites. The nest is usually no more than a depression in the ground, with little or no lining material in which between two and five (generally four) heavily marked eggs are laid. Golden plover nestlings *right* have very attractive golden-yellow mottled down which provides excellent camouflage.

The spur-winged plover *left* is a distinctive black and white bird which lives in south-eastern Europe, Egypt, Arabia and Africa. The Australian spur-winged plover *below* is a bird of open grasslands and can be recognised easily by its yellow facial wattle.

Pheasants

Man has enjoyed an intimate involvement with the pheasant family for longer than with any other group of birds. This large family of game birds includes the true pheasants, quails, partridges, peafowl and jungle fowl. They have provided sport as well as eggs and meat for the table; the domestic hen is descended from jungle fowl.

The common pheasant *left* is a bird of open country, farmland, woodland edges, hills and mountain slopes. It has been introduced into Britain, the United States, Japan and New Zealand from its native Asia.

Although the golden pheasant is a familiar bird in zoological gardens little is known about its habits in its native China and there is no record of its nest or eggs having been found in its homeland. It is a ground-dwelling bird with a preference for bamboo scrub on mountain and hill sides. If two cocks are placed in a confined space they will fight *right*.

Blood pheasants *below* live at high altitude near the snow line in Nepal, Tibet and north-west China.

45

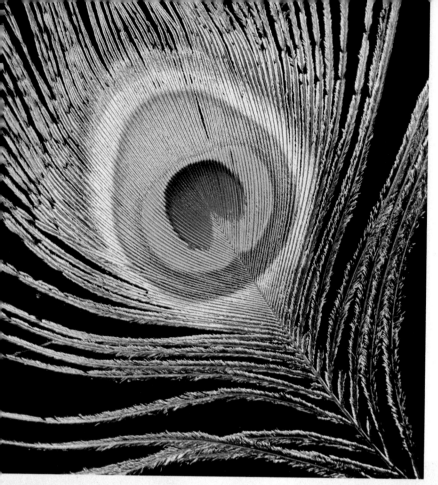

Peafowl

There are two species of peafowl or peacock, the blue peacock from India and Sri Lanka and the green peacock which comes from Burma, Indochina and Malaysia. The blue or Indian species has been domesticated for over 2,000 years without any significant change in shape or size; there have, however, been some plumage mutations such as that exhibited by these white birds *bottom left*. The cocks are striking birds with beautiful eyed trains (a feather is shown *top left*) which develop into huge shivering fans *right* when they perform their frontal display to hens. Captive birds which have no hens to display to become imprinted on people and put on the same elegant performance for them. Peafowl are birds of woodland and forest which forage for berries, buds, seeds, insects and grubs. The nest is built on the ground with a spartan lining of leaves or grass and four to eight large creamy-white or pale buff eggs are laid in it. The hen is an exemplary parent, caring for her young without any help from the cock. The chicks are so well developed when they hatch that within a few days they are able to fly up into the branches to roost with their mother.

Ratites

The name ratite is given to a number of flightless running birds, both living and extinct. The extinct species are the fabulous elephant birds of Madagascar and the moas of New Zealand. The elephant birds, as their name suggests, were very large, being as tall as the ostrich but bulkier; their eggs were huge, having a capacity of about nine litres. The last elephant bird perished in about 1649 and the largest of the moas, Dinornis, also vanished in the seventeenth century, exterminated by the Maoris. Cassowarys *right*, modern ratites, are shaped very like the extinct moas. These highly aggressive birds have powerful claws capable of killing a man. They live in the forests of Australia and New Guinea and can dash through the undergrowth at a speed of about fifty kilometres per hour.

There are three species of kiwi *left*, all of which are found in New Zealand. These shy, elusive birds forage at night; their long bills have the nostrils at the tips enabling them to locate insects, grubs and worms by scent. Kiwis nest

in burrows, the larger female usually laying a single chalky-white egg which is incubated by the male for a period of up to eighty days.

The emu *far left* is the second largest living ratite, standing nearly two metres high; it is widely distributed across Australia. Emus are excellent swimmers and very fast runners which, like the cassowary, can attain speeds of nearly fifty kilometres per hour. Early settlers used to kill these birds for their flesh, the flavour of which has been likened to that of beef, and a single egg would have been large enough to supply breakfast for a whole family.

The ostrich *below* is the largest bird living today. It stands over two metres high and weighs over 100 kilogrammes; altogether it is an impressive sight. Over recent years its numbers have been drastically reduced; in Arabia it has been totally eliminated and in some other regions it is so rare that sometimes only its tracks *below centre* are to be seen. The ostrich is well-known for its omnivorous habits and feeds on all kinds of plants and their fruits as well as on lizards, small tortoises and rodents. Captive birds have been known to consume nails, belts, coins and other unusual objects.

Hummingbirds

There are over 130 different species of hummingbird, all of which are restricted to the New World. These very small, incredibly fast birds can beat their wings up to seventy times per second, creating the sound which has given them their name. The bee hummingbird of Cuba is the smallest bird in the world; at only two and a half centimetres long it is the same size as a bumble bee. Hummingbirds are found in a variety of habitats including deserts, rain forests and the high slopes of mountains. They build neat, cupped nests using moss and lichen bound together with spiders' silk. Many hummingbirds, including the glittering-bellied emerald *left* and the common emerald *below* are found in South America. Anna's hummingbird *right* lives in California all the year round where it is often seen in gardens.

The Old World Sunbirds, such as the orange-breasted sunbird *far right* of southern Africa, are not related to the hummingbirds but are their counterparts, filling the same ecological niche in the Old World as that occupied by the hummingbirds in the New.

Kingfishers

These brightly-coloured birds which often have metallic-looking plumage are generally solitary in their behaviour, sitting silently waiting to pounce or dive on their unsuspecting prey. Kingfishers are stumpy, large-headed birds which are widely distributed, with the greatest concentration of species occurring in the Old World, particularly in Asia and the East Indies.

South of the Sahara the quiet streams, lakes and rivers of Africa are the home of the malachite kingfisher *right*. Although it is extremely brightly coloured its small size and its ability to remain motionless for long periods make it an easy bird to overlook. It lives exclusively on a diet of fish and other aquatic life and so does not compete with its smaller relative, the pygmy kingfisher *left*, which is essentially a woodland bird, feeding on crickets and other insects. The blue-winged kookaburra *bottom left* of northern Australia and New Guinea feeds on a variety of creatures including insects, crabs, lizards and frogs. The common European kingfisher *below* builds its nest by tunnelling with its bill into the sides of river banks, ejecting the loosened earth using its feet and tail.

Bee-eaters

Bee-eaters are among the most colourful of all birds; all twenty-four species are exceptionally graceful as they fly in pursuit of their insect prey which includes bees, wasps and butterflies. These Old World birds are widely distributed throughout southern Europe, Africa and Asia. In tropical America the long-billed jacamars fill a similar ecological niche with their aerial pursuit of insects and habit of nesting in burrows.

The European Bee-eater *left*, from the Mediterranean countries, Russia and North Africa, is the only member of the family found in the temperate region. Large noisy flocks migrate in autumn, moving south to Africa, and even to India, where they over-winter. In summer they nest in colonies; sometimes hundreds of breeding pairs congregate at one site where they dig tunnels up to three metres long. Four to eight white eggs are laid in the nesting chamber and both parents share in the incubation of the eggs and care of the young.

The white-throated bee-eater *top* is an exclusively African resident and inhabits the forest edge, woodland, savannah and desert bush areas of Senegal, Ethiopia, Uganda and Kenya. The carmine bee-eater *centre* also lives in Africa and is one of the most striking members of the family, having brilliant red and pale pink plumage and extremely long central tail feathers. Huge flocks numbering up to 1,000 birds assemble at the nesting sites which are usually sand cliffs close to water. Like their European relatives they make their nests in tunnels but they lay smaller clutches of two to four white eggs. They too feed on bees and wasps but are particularly fond of locusts and grasshoppers. Like all bee-eaters they need a look-out post and will frequently sit on the backs of ostriches, bustards, antelopes and cattle waiting for insects to be disturbed by their mobile perches. They are instinctively attracted to grassland fires where there is always a plentiful supply of insects.

One of the most widely-distributed of the bee-eaters is the little green bee-eater *bottom* which is found south of the Sahara and eastwards through Africa and Asia as far as southern China. Enjoying a varied habitat, it is quite at home 2,000 metres up in the hills, in the savannahs or in village gardens.

Parrots

The parrot family is a large one, containing well over three hundred different species of colourful, noisy and often quarrelsome characters. Parrots are widely distributed throughout South America, the Caribbean, Africa, Asia, Australasia and many of the oceanic islands. Many, like the yellow-fronted Amazon parrot *left*, are fruit-eaters but there are some which feed exclusively on fungi. The kea and kaka of New Zealand have often been accused of killing sheep; they use their long bills to tear at the fat and flesh of these animals.

The gold and blue macaw *right* is one of fifteen species of large powerful parrot which inhabit the rain forests of Mexico and Central and South America. They feed on a variety of fruits and their powerful beaks can easily split nuts open.

The African grey parrot *below* is a popular pet because of its remarkable ability to mimic the human voice. In the wild these fast-flying birds can be seen in noisy flocks flying high over forests; in some parts of Africa they have become an agricultural pest, attacking crops, particularly maize.

Eagles

The eagle family contains some of the most powerful of all the living birds. The Steller's sea eagle has a wing span of two and a half metres and can easily kill a large seal calf, while the fierce harpy eagle weaves through rain forests with incredible agility, picking off monkeys, sloths, porcupines and opossums. The open plains of Africa are the home of the bateleur eagle *left*, a powerful, stocky bird which in the air is transformed into a spectacular flying machine. It spends most of its time on the wing, gliding effortlessly and covering up to 300 or more kilometres a day. It engages in acrobatics, including side-rolls, which have to be seen to be believed, and its stoop as it rushes towards the ground has been described as sounding like the passage of a six inch shell. Although the bateleur eagle is primarily a scavenger it has been known to attack small antelope and molest larger raptors such as vultures and lammergeiers in an effort to persuade them to disgorge their food.

Golden eagles *right* may need as much as 100 square kilometres of territory for hunting purposes and they easily range over such large areas with their ability to fly at 200 kilometres per hour. During a stoop for a kill, or even just in play, they can reach speeds of 250-300 kilometres per hour. Mammals and game birds are the most important elements of their diet.

Unfortunately the bald eagle *bottom left*, emblem of the United States, has disappeared from most of its former range. The combined effects of shooting, destruction of nest sites, industrial pollution of rivers and the use of insecticides have taken a heavy toll. Bald eagles are fish eaters which do not put too much effort into obtaining a meal, preferring to scavenge or to harass the osprey to force it to release its catch. The African fish eagle *below* is another fish-eating raptor which can lift fish weighing up to two kilogrammes in its powerful talons.

Africa's Verreaux's eagle *far right* is a bird of rocks, hills and crags, which feeds mainly on mammals such as rock hyraxes, small antelope and hares.

Owls

The most striking feature of any owl is its eyes which are large and placed in the front of its head, rather like our own. This large size allows much of the available light to pass through, an important characteristic for a nocturnal creature. The frontal arrangement is a method of accommodating such large eyes and provides binocular vision. Owls' hearing is acute, enabling them to pin-point their prey even in total darkness.

The saw-whet owl *left* is a bird of damp, thick woodlands of North America which hunts at night and at twilight. It preys on small mammals including bats, as well as birds and amphibians. Snowy owls *right* are birds of the arctic tundra which often prey on lemmings but they are powerful enough to deal with ground squirrels and ducks and in coastal regions they catch a variety of sea-birds.

Tawny owls *below and far right* are the most vocal of all the European species; their hooting and 'ki-wik' calls are regular nightly sounds in woodlands and large gardens. This is very much a nocturnal species and if the tawny owl does venture out during the day it is mobbed by a host of other

birds. The owlets are fed by their parents for several weeks after they have left the nest and are aggressively protected; tawny owls will not hesitate to attack man in defence of their nest and young.

Long-eared owls *left and below* prefer coniferous woodlands and, being strictly nocturnal, they hide during the day by pressing themselves closely to tree trunks. When on the defensive they put on a formidable display which involves arching their wings while snapping, hissing and spitting.

The barn owl *right* is a widely-distributed species which is found in North and South America, Europe, Russia, Africa, Asia and Australia. This wide distribution coupled with its distinctive whitish appearance probably makes it the best known of all the owls. When hunting it searches over moorland, grassland and farmland for rats, mice, young rabbits, shrews and voles and will also kill small birds when these are flushed from their roosting places. This prey is generally devoured whole. Barn owls prefer to use buildings such as churches, barns, lofts and other out-buildings for nesting, where they do not build a nest as such but lay their white eggs, between three and seven in each clutch, in a crevice or depression.

INDEX

Page numbers refer to illustrations

Published 1987 by Colour Library Books Ltd,
Guildford, Surrey, England.
© 1987 Colour Library Ltd.
© Illustrations: Bruce Coleman Ltd.
Printed and bound in Barcelona, Spain by Cronion, S.A.
All rights reserved.
ISBN 0 904681 55 6

Dep. Leg. B-14840-87